Four Friends Tell Stories about Jesus

Allan R. Bevere

Energion Publications
Cantonment, Florida
2024

Copyright © 2024, Allan R. Bevere. All Rights Reserved

Image Credits:

Adobe Stock: 4, 12, 13, 24, 30, 32, 34, 37, 61, 63, 65, 68, 75, 80, 83, 85, 89, 92, 96, 99, 102, 106, 109

iStockPhoto.com: 43, 49, 54, 59, 70

Boy Jesus in the Temple — Illustration 163216438 © Patrick Guenette | Dreamstime.com

Generated with Adobe Firefly AI: Title page background, 11, 18, 21, 47, 56, 93

Cover Images: Background — Adobe Stock; 4 apostle figures — iStockPhoto.com

ISBN: 978-1-63199-905-5

eISBN: 978-1-63199-906-2

Energion Publications

1241 Conference Rd

Cantonment, FL 32533

pubs@energion.com

energion.com

(850) 525-3916

For my granddaughters

Aly, Emery, Quinn, and Spencer

May the story of Jesus be their story.

THE STORIES

A Special Word to the Grown Ups 7

Jesus' Four Special Friends—Matthew, Mark, Luke, and John 10

The Shepherds Meet the Newborn Jesus (Luke 2:1-20) 13

The Wise Men Visit the Child Jesus (Matthew 2:1-11) 16

The Boy Jesus Teaches in the Temple (Luke 2:41-52) 19

John Baptizes Jesus (Mark 1:1-11) 22

Jesus Is Tempted (Matthew 4:1-11) 25

Jesus Calls His First **Disciples** (Matthew 4:12-22) 27

Jesus Turns Water into Wine (John 2:1-11) 29

Jesus Frees a Person from Demons (Mark 5:11-20) 31

Jesus and Nicodemus (John 3:1-16) 33

Jesus Teaches about the World Where God is King (Matthew 5:1-16) 35

Jesus Heals a Man Who Cannot Walk (Luke 5:17-26) 38

The Farmer Scatters Seed (Mark 4:1-9, 14-20) 40

Jesus and a Samaritan Woman (John 4:4-42) 44

Living Wisely (Matthew 11:16-19) 46

Having Great Faith (Luke 7:1-10) 48

Jesus Walks on Water (Matthew 14:22-33) 50

Jesus Helps a Woman and a Girl (Mark 6:21-43) 52

Who Do You Say that I Am? (Mark 8:27-33) 55

The Man Who Could Not Walk (John 5:1-16) 57

Jesus Praises John the Baptist (Matthew 11:2-11) 60

Jesus Calms the Storm (Luke 8:22-25) 62
The Transfiguration of Jesus (Luke 9:28-36) 64
Jesus Teaches His Friends How to Pray (Luke 11:1-13) 66
Jesus **Blesses** the Children (Mark 10:13-16) 69
A Question of Greatness (Mark 35-45) 71
Jesus Feeds 5000 People (John 6:1-14) 73
Jesus Heals a Man Born Blind (John 9:1-38) 76
Jesus Raises His Friend Lazarus (John 11:1-44) 79
Ten Bridesmaids and Their Lamps (Matthew 25:1-13) 81
The Sheep and the Goats (Matthew 25:31-46) 84
Mary **Anoints** Jesus' Feet (John 12:1-8) 86
A Big Parade! (John 12:12-19) 88
Jesus Washes his **Disciples**' Feet (John 13:1-20) 90
The Last Supper (Mark 14:12-32) 93
Jesus Is Betrayed, Arrested, Denied, and Put on Trial (Luke 22:39-23:25) 95
Jesus Is **Crucified** on a Cross (Matthew 27:27-61) 98
Jesus is Alive Again! (Mark 16:1-8) 101
The Risen Jesus Appears to Two **Disciples** (Luke 24:13-35) 103
Jesus Ascends to Heaven (Acts 1:6-11) 107

A Special Word to the Grown Ups

I have always written for adults. It never occurred to me to write for children. But when your eight-year-old granddaughter says to you, "Gramps, you should write a book of Bible stories kids can understand," how could I refuse?

This book is the result of my granddaughter's suggestion. I hope it is indeed a book of Bible stories kids can understand, but I also know that adults have an indispensable role in helping them understand. Please take the time to read these stories with them. As we know, children have many questions. As Jesus journeyed with his first followers, they had plenty of questions for him. I hope families will use these stories on the journey of faith. Walk with your children, grandchildren, nieces, and nephews through these pages together. Following Jesus on the road of life is best when travelled together. Children need your guidance.

We know that Jesus and his **disciples** were first century Jews—Semites from the Middle East. Historically, they were more darkly complected than white Europeans, though we cannot know the exact shade. Portraying Jesus mostly as a Caucasian throughout Western history has been unfortunate, and it is a good thing that correctives can now be found.

Theologically, however, we know that Jesus is for everybody regardless of skin color. Many years ago, when I was a young college student, I traveled to Haiti to do some short-term mission work. One Saturday, we tool a break from our labors and visited downtown Port-au-Prince, the nation's capital. We entered an historic church and on the walls of the sanctuary were painted scenes depicting various events in the life of Jesus. For the first time in my life, I was seeing representations of Jesus and his **disciples** as black. It had never occurred to me that Jesus might not be white. Regardless of Jesus' actual skin tone, it made perfect sense for the Haitian people to present the biblical characters as they themselves looked. Ninety-five percent of all Haitians are of African descent.

There is a song sung at Christmas that makes the point well.

> Some children see him
> Lily white
> The baby Jesus
> Born this night
> Some children see him
> Lily white
> With tresses soft
> And fair

Some children see him
Bronzed and brown
The Lord of heav'n
To Earth come down
Some children see him
Bronzed and brown
With dark
And heavy hair

Some children see him
Almond-eyed
This savior whom
We kneel beside
Some children see him
Almond-eyed
With skin
Of yellow hue

Some children see him
Dark as they
Sweet Mary's son
To whom we pray
Some children see him
Dark as they
And, ah
They love him, too

The children
In each diff'rent place
Will see
The baby Jesus' face
Like theirs
But bright
With heav'nly grace
And filled
With holy light

O lay aside
Each earthly thing
And with thy heart
As offering
Come worship now
The infant king
'Tis love
That's born tonight[1]

With that in mind, I asked my publisher to choose illustrations of Jesus portrayed as an ethnically diverse individual. In these pages you will encounter a Jesus illustrated as European, African, Asian, Latin American, and from other places around the world. I want every child who reads this book to see their face in the face of Jesus. Illustrations include some partially generated with AI, and those are indicated on the copyright page.

At the end of this book is a glossary that defines words used in the book in ways children can understand. This is another place where grownups can assist children in learning about the faith. I am sure I have unconsciously omitted some terms, but I hope most of the important words have been included. Glossary words are printed in bold throughout the book. Other words like "baptism" are explained in one or more of the stories.

Finally, I wish to thank Henry and Jody Neufeld, my publishers who are always ready to consider my crazy ideas in a serious way. They are a delight to work with in the world of publishing. I also wish to thank my friend and colleague, Reverend Lindsey Funtik for proofreading and offering valuable suggestions in making this book better. For the foreseeable future, I owe her endless cups of java at our favorite coffee shop.

---

1   History of Hymns: "Some Children See Him," https://www.umcdiscipleship.org/articles/history-of-hymns-some-children-see-him.
Or find on YouTube: https://youtu.be/s49gEmTlOTk?si=qP2QSoOc7TjBaE92 (James Taylor)
https://youtu.be/QMOkL8BfbwU?si=NKaSqV3P0qK3mHCl (Bebe Winans)

Jesus' Four Special Friends—Matthew, Mark, Luke, and John

The Gospels are books in the Bible that tell us about the life of Jesus. They were written by four different people: Matthew, Mark, Luke, and John. Each of them had their own special way of telling stories about what Jesus said and did.

Matthew was one of Jesus' followers. He was also one of his Twelve **Apostles**. The **Apostles** were Jesus' very first followers. Matthew wrote his Gospel to show how Jesus fulfilled the prophecies from the **Old Testament**. He talked about Jesus' birth, his teachings, and the **miracles** he performed. Matthew wanted people to know that Jesus was the promised Messiah, the one who would save people from their **sins**.

Mark was a friend of the **Apostle** Peter, who was also one of Jesus' first followers. Mark wrote his Gospel to show how Jesus was a servant and a healer. He talked about Jesus' actions and how he helped people who were sick or in trouble. Mark wanted people to see that Jesus was full of compassion and that he cared for everyone.

Luke was a doctor and a friend of the **Apostle** Paul, who also followed Jesus. Luke wrote his Gospel to give information about what really happened during Jesus' life. He talked about Jesus' birth, his teachings, and the many people he met along the way. Luke wanted to make sure that people understood the true story of Jesus and how he came to save the world.

The **Apostle** John was another one of Jesus' followers, and he wrote his Gospel to focus on the spiritual side of Jesus. John talked about how Jesus was both really human and really God. He shared stories about Jesus' love and how he showed people the way to God. John wanted people to know that Jesus was the light of the world and that through him, they could find eternal life.

So, the Gospels of Matthew, Mark, Luke, and John tell us about the amazing life of Jesus: his teachings, death, and **resurrection** and the love he had for people. They are important books that help us understand who Jesus is and how much he cares for each one of us. Every story in this book comes from the Gospels.

The Shepherds Meet the Newborn Jesus (Luke 2:1-20)

Jesus was going to be born in a little town called Bethlehem, but his parents, Mary and Joseph had to travel there from their home in Nazareth. They had to go because there was something important taking place.

Now, the ruler of the land, Caesar Augustus wanted to know how many people lived in his kingdom, so he ordered everyone to go to their hometown to be counted. That is why Mary and Joseph had to go to Bethlehem.

Mary and Joseph journeyed, and when they arrived in Bethlehem they discovered that many other people had come there too. Mary was going to have her baby soon, so they needed a place to rest.

When they went to their relative's house, the only room they could find was the one where animals, like cows and sheep, were kept. They made a cozy bed for Mary in the straw, and that is where Jesus was born that night.

In the fields nearby, there were shepherds taking care of their sheep. Suddenly, an angel appeared in the sky shining with bright light. The shepherds were scared at first, but the angel told them not to be afraid because he had good news for them.

The angel said, "Do not be afraid! I bring you good news of great joy that will be for all the people. Today in the town of David, a Savior has been born to you; he is Christ the Lord! You will find the baby wrapped in blankets and lying in a manger."

After the angel finished speaking, many angels appeared in the sky praising God and saying, "Praise to God in the highest, and on earth peace, goodwill toward everyone!"

The shepherds were amazed and excited by the angel's message. They decided to go to Bethlehem and see this special baby. They found the stable where Mary, Joseph, and baby Jesus were. They told them about the angels and how they had come to see the baby because the angel said he was the Savior.

The shepherds were filled with joy and wonder as they looked at the baby Jesus. They knew that something incredible had happened. They praised God for sending Jesus to be the Savior of the world.

Word about Jesus' birth began to spread, and many people were amazed at this special baby. The shepherds went back to their fields, praising and glorifying God for all they had seen and heard.

And that is the story of how Jesus, the Savior was born in Bethlehem and how the shepherds came to see him. It reminds us that Jesus came to bring joy and peace to the world, and his birth is a reason for us to celebrate and be thankful.

The Wise Men Visit the Child Jesus (Matthew 2:1-11)

When Jesus was born there were some very special people called wise men. These wise men were very good at studying the stars and learning about the world. One night, as they were looking up at the sky they saw a very bright star shining brightly.

The wise men knew that this star was a sign of something amazing happening. They believed it meant that a very special baby was going to be born, a baby who would bring great joy to the world. They were so excited and decided to follow the star to find this special baby.

So, the wise men gathered their things and set off on a long journey. They traveled through deserts and over mountains following the star that led the way. They were determined to find this baby and give him special gifts.

After traveling for many days, the wise men arrived in a little town called Bethlehem. They went to the king of that land, named Herod the Great, and asked him where they could find the baby who was born to be the king of the

Jews. The king was surprised and did not know about this special baby, so he asked his advisors.

The advisors told the king that the baby was born in Bethlehem, just as the **prophet** had foretold. King Herod told the wise men to go and find the baby and then come back and tell the him where he was so that he could go and worship the baby too. The wise men were happy to know they were getting closer to the baby.

So, the wise men continued their journey and followed the star until it stopped above a humble little house. They were overjoyed! They went inside and saw the baby, who was just as the star had told them. The wise men fell down on their knees and worshiped the baby.

The wise men then gave the baby three special gifts: gold, frankincense, and myrrh. Gold was a precious metal fit for a king, frankincense was a lovely smelling perfume used in worship, and myrrh was a special oil used for **anointing**. These gifts were meant to show honor and love for the baby.

After spending some time with the baby, the wise men knew it was time to go back home. But they did not go back to the king as he had asked. They had a dream warning them not to, so they took a different route and returned to their own country.

The wise men were filled with joy and wonder at what they had seen. They knew that this baby, Jesus, was no ordinary baby. He was the promised king, the one who would bring love, peace, and joy to the world. And they were grateful to have been a part of his story.

And so, the wise men's journey came to an end, but the story of Jesus, the special baby was just beginning. The wise men's visit was a reminder that Jesus came to bring hope and love to everyone, no matter who they were or where they came from. And that is a story that we still celebrate every Christmas.

The Boy Jesus Teaches in the Temple (Luke 2:41-52)

Jesus lived with his parents, Mary and Joseph, in a town called Nazareth. They were a happy family, and they loved each other very much.

One day, when Jesus was about 12 years old his family went on a trip to Jerusalem. They went there to celebrate a special holiday called Passover. Many people from different places came to Jerusalem to celebrate together.

After the Passover celebration, Jesus' family started to head back home. But something happened—they realized that Jesus was not with them! Mary and Joseph were worried and began searching for him everywhere.

They looked and looked, asking their relatives and friends if they had seen Jesus. Finally, after three days of searching, they found him in the temple in Jerusalem. Jesus was sitting among the teachers, listening and asking them questions.

When Mary and Joseph saw Jesus, they were both relieved and a little bit upset. Mary asked Jesus, "Why did you do this to us? We were so worried!" Jesus replied, "Why were you looking for me? Did not you know that I must be in my Heavenly Father's house?"

Jesus' parents did not understand what he meant, but they loved him and knew that he was a special child. They took him back home to Nazareth, and Jesus continued to grow in wisdom and strength. He was loved by God and by the people around him.

This story teaches us that Jesus was not an ordinary boy. He had a special connection with God, and even at a young age, he had wisdom beyond his years. It also shows us the importance of family and how Mary and Joseph cared deeply for Jesus.

So, remember no matter how young or old we are, we can all learn from Jesus' example of love, wisdom, and respect for our parents.

John Baptizes Jesus (Mark 1:1-11)

There was a man named John who lived a long, long time ago. He was a special person chosen by God to tell everyone about someone very important who was coming.

One day, John went to a place called the wilderness, which was a big, open area with no houses or buildings. People from all around came to see and hear him because they knew he had something important to say.

John was dressed differently. He wore clothes made from camel hair and had a leather belt around his waist. He ate strange food like locusts (which are bugs. Yuck!) and wild honey. But he was not there to talk about his clothes or food. He had a much more important message.

John told the people, "Get ready! Someone amazing is coming soon, someone who is even more important than me. I am just here to prepare the way for him."

He said that people needed to change their ways and stop doing bad things. John asked them to confess their **sins** and be baptized in the water as a sign of starting fresh and being ready for the special person who was coming.

Many people came forward and were baptized by John in the river. (That is why he was called John the Baptist or John the Baptizer.) The people were baptized to show that they were sorry for the wrong things they had done and that they wanted to follow God's ways.

John also told the people that the special person who was coming would be much greater than him. He said, "I baptize you with water, but he will baptize you with the Holy Spirit."

John wanted everyone to understand that the one who was coming was the Son of God, Jesus. He was going to bring good news, love, and forgiveness to the world.

But then, something amazing happened! Jesus himself came to John to be baptized. Can you imagine that? The Son of God being baptized by John!

As Jesus was coming out of the water, something incredible happened. The heavens opened, and the Holy Spirit, who is God's special person that gives people God's special presence, came down on Jesus like a dove. It was a beautiful and magical moment.

And then, a voice from heaven said, "You are my beloved Son; with you, I am well pleased." It was God himself speaking! He was telling everyone that Jesus was his special Son and that He loved Him very much.

Jesus came to show us God's love and teach us how to live in a way that pleases God. He came to save us from our **sin**s and give us new life.

Jesus Is Tempted
(Matthew 4:1-11)

Jesus had just been baptized in the Jordan River by his cousin John. The Spirit of God came down from heaven like a dove and rested on Jesus.

After this incredible experience, Jesus felt led by the Spirit to go into the wilderness. He wanted to spend some time alone with God and prepare himself for the special work he had to do.

Jesus went without food for forty days and forty nights, which is a long time! He was hungry and weak, and that is when a sneaky character called the devil showed up. The devil wanted to test Jesus and try to make him do things that were not right.

The devil said to Jesus, "If you are really the Son of God, then you can turn these stones into bread and eat." The devil wanted Jesus to use his special powers for himself and take the easy way out. But Jesus knew it was not right to do something just to satisfy his own needs. So, he answered, "People shall not live by bread alone, but by every word that comes from the mouth of God."

Then, the devil took Jesus to a very high place and said, "If you jump off, the **angels** will save you because God will protect you." The devil was trying to make Jesus show off his power and do something dangerous. But Jesus knew that testing God in that way was not right. So, he said, "You shall not put the Lord your God to the test."

Finally, the devil took Jesus to a mountain and showed him all the kingdoms of the world. He said, "If you worship me, I will give you all of this." The devil wanted Jesus to worship him instead of God. But Jesus knew that only God deserved worship and honor. So, he said, "Be gone, Satan! For it is written, 'You shall worship the Lord your God and him only shall you serve.'"

When the devil saw that Jesus did not give in to his temptations, he left him alone. **Angels** came and took care of Jesus, giving him strength and comfort after his time in the wilderness.

This story shows us that even though Jesus faced difficult temptations, he always chose to do what was right. It teaches us the importance of listening to God's words and following them, even when we are tempted to do something wrong.

Jesus Calls His First Disciples (Matthew 4:12-22)

When Jesus was a grown up, he moved to a place called Capernaum. Capernaum was a city near a big lake called the Sea of Galilee.

When Jesus arrived in Capernaum, he saw two brothers, Simon (who was also called Peter) and Andrew. They were fishermen, and they were working by the lake trying to catch fish with their nets.

Jesus walked up to them and said something amazing. He told them, "Come with me, and I will make you fishers of people.' Jesus was not talking about catching fish anymore. He was talking about helping people and spreading his message of love and kindness.

Guess what? Simon and Andrew were so inspired by Jesus' words that they immediately left their fishing nets and decided to follow him. They became his **disciples**, which means they became his special friends and helpers. They became his followers.

But the story does not end there. Jesus kept walking along the shore, and he saw two more brothers, James and John. They were also fishermen, and they were in a boat with their father, mending their nets.

Just like with Simon and Andrew, Jesus called out to James and John. He also asked them to come with him and become fishers of people. And guess what? Just like Simon and Andrew, James and John were so inspired by Jesus that they left their fishing boat and their father and decided to follow Jesus too.

So now, Jesus had four followers called **disciples** (they were also called **apostles**)—Simon (Peter), Andrew, James, and John. They all left their fishing jobs behind to be with Jesus and help him with his mission.

Jesus called ordinary people like fishermen to be his friends and helpers. He wanted them to spread his message of God's love and kindness to other people. It shows us that Jesus wants all of us, no matter who we are, to follow him and help others in our own special ways.

Jesus Turns Water into Wine (John 2:1-11)

In town of Cana, there was a special party happening. It was a wedding. Jesus and his friends were invited to the wedding, and it was going to be a lot of fun.

But something happened that was not so good. The people running the party realized they had run out of something very important. They did not have any more wine for the guests to drink. This was a big problem because wine was a common drink at weddings, and it would have been embarrassing if they did not have any left.

But Jesus' mother, Mary knew that Jesus could help. She asked him to do something about it. Jesus listened to his mother and wanted to help, even though he was not sure what to do at first.

Nearby, there were six big jars made of stone. Jesus told the people in charge to fill the jars with water. They did what he asked, even though they probably did not understand why.

Then, something amazing happened! When the servants poured out the water from the jars and gave it to the person in charge of the party to taste, it had turned into wine! Not just any wine, but good and tasty wine!

The person in charge of the party was surprised because usually the best wine was served first, and then the less expensive wine served later. But in this case, the best wine had come last! It was like Jesus had saved the best for the end.

Everyone at the party was happy. Jesus had turned water into wine, and it was a wonderful surprise. This was one of the **miracles** Jesus did to show his power and love for people.

Jesus Frees a Person from Demons (Mark 5:11-20)

There was a man who lived in a place called Gadara. But this man was not like other people. He had some problems and was not feeling well. People in the town feared him because he did strange things and acted differently.

One day, Jesus came to Gadara with his friends. When the man saw Jesus, he ran towards him. The man knew that Jesus was a very special person, and he wanted to be near him. But Jesus saw that the man was not feeling well and he wanted to help him.

Jesus talked to the man and asked him his name. The man said his name was "Legion" because he had many problems inside him. He had a lot of bad thoughts and feelings.

There were some pigs nearby, and the demons inside the man asked Jesus if they could go into the pigs. Jesus agreed, and all the bad things inside the man went into the pigs. The pigs then ran off a cliff and into the water.

When the people in the town saw this, they were amazed and a little scared too. They told everyone what happened, and people came to see Jesus and the man. The man was now completely fine. He was not doing strange things anymore. He was calm and happy because Jesus helped him.

Jesus and his friends had to leave Gadara after that, but the man wanted to go with them. But Jesus said, "No, you go back to your home and tell everyone about the good things God has done for you." So, the man went back to his town and told everyone how Jesus had helped him and made him better.

This story teaches us that Jesus has the power to heal people and take away their troubles. It also shows us that no matter how different or troubled we may feel, Jesus loves us and can help us too.

Jesus and Nicodemus (John 3:1-16)

Nicodemus was very curious and wanted to know more about Jesus. So, one night, he went to meet Jesus secretly.

When Nicodemus found Jesus, he said, "Teacher, we know that you are from God because you do amazing things." He wanted to understand how Jesus could do all those **miracles**.

Jesus replied, "Nicodemus, to truly understand what I do you must be born again." Nicodemus was puzzled and asked, "How can a person be born again? Can they enter their mother again and be born all over?"

Nicodemus did not understand. Being born again means starting a new life with God. It is like when a caterpillar becomes a beautiful butterfly. You see, God loves us so much that he wants us to have a new life with him.

Jesus continued, "God sent me, his only Son, to bring this new life to everyone. Whoever believes in me will not be separated from God but will have eternal life."

Nicodemus listened carefully trying to understand. Jesus told him, "God loves the world so much that he sent me, not to judge people, but to save them. Whoever believes in me will have eternal life and be with God forever."

Jesus explained that this new life comes from believing in him, just like we believe that the sun will rise every morning. God's love is like a bright light shining in the darkness, and when we believe in Jesus that light shines in our hearts.

Nicodemus was amazed and grateful for Jesus' words. He realized that Jesus was not just an ordinary man but someone very special, sent by God to bring hope and love to everyone.

From that day on, Nicodemus understood that he needed to have faith in Jesus and accept his love. He knew that by believing in Jesus, he could have a new life, free from **sin**, and full of God's love.

The story of Nicodemus teaches us that by believing in Jesus and accepting his love, we can have a new life and be with God forever. Just like a caterpillar transforms into a butterfly, we can be transformed by God's love and have eternal life with Him.

Jesus Teaches about the World Where God is King (Matthew 5:1-16)

One day, Jesus went up a mountain. His friends followed him to the top.

Jesus sat down and began to teach them. He said, "God blesses those who realize they need him. They will live in a world where God is king."

"God **blesses** those who are sad. He will comfort them and make them feel better."

"God **blesses** those who are gentle and kind. They will **inherit** many good things."

"God **blesses** those who always want to do the right thing. They will be filled with joy."

"God **blesses** those who truly want to be close to him. They will feel his presence."

"God **blesses** those who show **mercy** and forgive others. He will show **mercy** to them too."

"God **blesses** those whose hearts are pure. They will see and know God."

"God **blesses** those who make peace. They will be called his children."

"God **blesses** those who are treated badly because they follow him. They will have a special place in heaven."

"People may say mean things about you because of me. But be happy and **rejoice** because you will have a great reward in heaven."

"You are like a light in the world. Let your light shine so that others can see the good things you do. And they will praise God because of you."

Jesus said, "You are like salt found underground. Salt adds flavor to food. You can make the world a better place by being good and kind to others."

"You are like a city on a hill. Everyone can see you and the good things you do. Shine brightly and be a good example for others."

"No one lights a lamp and puts it under a basket. Instead, they put it on a table so it can give light to everyone in the room."

Jesus said, "In the same way, let your light shine for others. Let them see the good things you do, and they will praise God."

Jesus Heals a Man Who Cannot Walk (Luke 5:17-26)

One day, Jesus was teaching a lot of people. They were gathered around him, listening to his words. They were so interested in what he had to say, that there was no more room inside the house where Jesus was speaking. Even the area outside the house was full of people trying to hear him.

While Jesus was teaching, four friends of a man who could not walk came up with an idea. They wanted to bring their friend to Jesus so that he could help him. But because there were so many people, they could not get through the door to reach Jesus.

The friends did not give up. They thought of a clever plan. They climbed up onto the roof of the house where Jesus was and made a hole in it. Can you imagine that? They lowered their friend down through the hole in the roof right in front of Jesus!

When Jesus saw the man, he knew he had great faith in God. Jesus knew that the man's friends believed that he could help their friend. So, Jesus did something amazing. He said to the man, "Your **sins** are forgiven."

Some religious leaders who were there got upset when they heard Jesus say that. They thought only God could forgive **sins**, and they did not believe Jesus was God. They thought he was saying something wrong.

But Jesus knew what they were thinking, and he asked them, "Which is easier: to say, 'Your **sin**s are forgiven,' or to say, 'Get up and walk'?" Jesus wanted to show them that he had the power to do both.

Then, Jesus said to the man who could not walk, "I say to you, get up, take your mat, and go home." And just like that, the man got up on his own two feet, picked up his mat, and went home! Everyone was amazed and praised God for what they had seen.

So, the story teaches us that Jesus has the power to heal and forgive **sins**. It also shows us the importance of having faith in Jesus and the love and determination of the friends who helped the man.

The Farmer Scatters Seed (Mark 4:1-9, 14-20)

Not only did Jesus' four friends, Matthew, Mark, Luke, and John like to tell stories, Jesus himself told stories. Jesus used stories as a way to tell people about the kingdom of God. The kingdom of God is another way of talking about the world where God is king.

Jesus often told stories to a big crowd of people who came to listen to him. Here is one of those stories.

He says, "Listen! A farmer went out to plant some seeds. As he scattered the seeds on the ground, some fell on a path, and the birds came and ate them up. Other seeds fell on rocky ground, where there was not much soil. These seeds sprouted quickly, but because they did not have deep roots, they dried up in the sun. Some seeds fell among thorns, and the thorns grew up and choked them. But some seeds fell on good soil and grew into healthy plants. They produced a lot of grain, some even a hundred times more than what was planted!"

So, what do Jesus' words mean? Let's imagine you are a farmer. You have some seeds, and you want to plant them to grow some plants. You go to your field and start scattering the seeds all around. Some of the seeds fall on a path where people walk, and the birds come and eat them. These seeds do not get a chance to grow into plants because they are quickly taken away.

Other seeds fall on rocky ground where there is not much soil. These seeds grow quickly, but because the soil is shallow, they cannot get enough water and nourishment to survive. So, they wither away and die.

Some seeds fall among thorns. Now, thorns are like those prickly plants. Thorns grow up and choke the seeds, which means the plants cannot grow properly because the thorns take all the nutrients and sunlight for themselves.

But some seeds fall on good soil. Good soil is rich, healthy dirt that has all the nutrients plants need to grow. These seeds find a nice spot in the soil, they get plenty of water and sunlight, and they grow into healthy plants that produce a lot of grain.

So, Jesus is saying that just like the different types of soil affect how well the seeds grow, our hearts can be like different types of soil. If our hearts are hard like the path, then when we hear good things, they do not really sink in, and we fail to understand or remember them.

If our hearts are like rocky ground, we might get excited about something for a little while, but if we do not keep learning and growing, we will not be able to stick with it when things get difficult.

If our hearts are like thorny soil, we might let worries or other things distract us from what is important, and it becomes hard to grow in our faith and do the right things.

But if our hearts are like good soil, then when we hear good things and learn about Jesus, we understand them and keep them in our hearts. We let them grow and make a positive difference in our lives. We become more loving, kind, and helpful to others.

Jesus and a Samaritan Woman (John 4:4-42)

There was a woman who lived in a place called Samaria. She needed water to drink and do her daily chores. One day, she went to a well to get some water. Now, this well was a special place because it had a lot of history. It was the well of a very famous person known by God's people. His name was Jacob. Jacob's well was a place where people would come to get water and talk to each other.

While the woman was at the well, a man came to her. Jesus asked the woman if she could give him some water to drink. The woman was surprised because Jesus was a Jewish man, and she was a Samaritan woman. In those days, Jewish and Samaritan people did not usually talk to each other.

But Jesus was different. He wanted to show the woman that he cared about her and her life. He told her something special. He said that if she knew who he was, she would ask him for something even more amazing than water.

The woman was curious and asked Jesus what he meant. Jesus told her that he was the Messiah, the special person that God had promised to send to save people. He told her that anyone who believed in him would have everlasting life.

The woman was amazed by what Jesus said. She believed him and wanted to share this incredible news with others. She left her water jar behind and ran back to her village. She told everyone she met about Jesus and invited them to come and see him for themselves.

The people from the village listened to the woman and were curious about Jesus. They went to see him and heard his words. Many of them believed in him too, just like the woman did. They realized that Jesus was the **Savior** they had been waiting for.

So, in this story we learn that Jesus cares about all people, no matter who they are or where they come from. He offers us something even more special than water. He offers us the chance to have an eternal friendship with God and to live with him forever.

Just like the woman in the story, we can also tell others about Jesus and share the good news with them. We can invite them to know him and experience his love and forgiveness.

Living Wisely (Matthew 11:16-19)

Jesus was talking to some people and trying to explain something important to them. He said, "What can I compare this generation to? They are like children sitting in the marketplaces and calling out to each other."

Imagine you and your friends are playing in a big market. You are sitting together and having fun. Jesus was saying that the people he was talking to were like children in a market, calling out to each other, just like you might do when they are playing a game or having a conversation.

One group of children said to the other group, "We played the flute for you, but you did not dance; we sang a sad song, but you did not cry." He was telling them that sometimes people try to make others happy by playing happy music, but these people did not want to dance. And sometimes people sing sad songs to make others feel better when they're sad, but these people did not want to cry.

Jesus was trying to show his listeners that no matter what he or other people did, they still did not want to listen and understand. He compared them to children who sometimes do not want to join in the fun or feel sad even when they're supposed to.

Then Jesus said something important: "**Wisdom**, that is knowing the ways of God, is shown to be right by what its followers do." He meant that wise people show they are smart by the things they do. It is not just about listening to good advice or saying the right things, but it is also about doing the right things.

So, in simple terms, Jesus was trying to teach the people that it is important to pay attention and understand the important things in life. It is not enough to just listen; we should also try to do what is right and make good choices. Just like how children playing together sometimes do not join in the fun or feel sad when they are supposed to, these people were not paying attention and not doing the right things. Jesus wanted them to understand the importance of **wisdom** and following it in their lives.

Having Great Faith (Luke 7:1-10)

Jesus could do amazing things, like healing sick people and even bringing them back to life!

One day, a man who was a soldier came to Jesus. He was worried because his servant was very sick and in much pain. The soldier cared a lot about his servant and wanted him to get better.

The soldier asked some people to go to Jesus and ask for his help. When Jesus heard about the soldier's servant, he decided to go and help them.

But before Jesus could reach the soldier's house, the soldier sent some of his friends to talk to Jesus. He said, "I am not worthy for you to come into my house. Just say the word, and my servant will be healed."

Jesus was amazed by the soldier's faith. Faith means believing that something will happen, even if we cannot see it. Jesus said, "I have not found such great faith even in Israel!"

And do you know what happened next? When the soldier's friends went back to the house, they found the servant completely healed! The soldier's faith in Jesus had made his servant well again.

This story teaches us that we can have faith in Jesus and believe that he can help us, just like the soldier believed. Even though we cannot see Jesus with our eyes, we can trust that he is there for us and can do amazing things in our lives.

So, just like the soldier, we can talk to Jesus and ask him for help when we need it. He loves us very much and wants to help us, just like he helped the soldier and his servant.

Jesus Walks on Water
(Matthew 14:22-33)

One day, Jesus told his friends to go ahead of him and get into a boat while he stayed behind to pray. The friends did what Jesus said and hopped into the boat.

Now, when evening came a big storm started to blow! The wind was strong, and the waves were crashing against the boat. Jesus could see his friends struggling in the storm from the shore, so he decided to help them.

But instead of getting into another boat or swimming, Jesus did something incredible. He walked on the water! He walked on top of the big waves as if they were solid ground. His friends in the boat could not believe their eyes. They were scared and thought it was a ghost!

But Jesus called out to them, saying, "Do not be afraid! It is me, Jesus!" His friends recognized his voice and were relieved.

Then, Peter who was one of Jesus' friends said, "Lord, if it is really you, tell me to come to you on the water."

Jesus replied, "Come, Peter!"

So, Peter bravely stepped out of the boat and began walking on the water toward Jesus. He was doing something amazing, just like Jesus! Peter was filled with joy and excitement.

However, as Peter looked around at the strong wind and the big waves, he became scared. He started to doubt and began sinking into the water. He cried out, "Lord, save me!"

Jesus immediately reached out his hand and caught Peter. He said, "You have such little faith. Why did you doubt?" Then Jesus helped Peter back into the boat, and the storm suddenly stopped.

Everyone in the boat was amazed and realized that Jesus truly was the Son of God. (The Heavenly Father had a very special relationship with Jesus. That is why he is called God's Son.) The **disciples** worshipped him and thanked him for saving them from the storm.

The story teaches us that when we trust Jesus and have faith in him, we can do incredible things. But sometimes, just like Peter we might doubt or get scared. When that happens, Jesus is always there to help us and lift us up, just like he did for Peter in the storm.

Jesus Helps a Woman and a Girl (Mark 6:21-43)

One day, Jesus went to a place called Capernaum and a big crowd gathered around him. People loved to listen to Jesus because he taught them about the ways of God: love, kindness, and how to be good to each other.

As Jesus was talking, a man came up to him. This man had a little girl who was very sick. He begged Jesus to come and help his daughter because he knew Jesus could heal her.

Jesus felt compassion for the man and agreed to go with him. Many people from the crowd followed Jesus and the man to his house, curious to see what would happen.

On the way to the man's house, something extraordinary happened. A woman who had been sick for many years came up to Jesus. She believed that if she could just touch his clothes, she would be healed.

So, she reached out and touched the edge of Jesus' robe. Immediately, she felt better! Her sickness was gone, and she was healed.

Jesus realized that someone had touched him, and he asked, "Who touched my clothes?" The woman came forward, scared but grateful and told Jesus what had happened.

Jesus smiled kindly at her and said, "Your faith has healed you. Go in peace."

Meanwhile, messengers arrived from the man's house and said, "Your daughter has died. There is no need to trouble Jesus anymore."

But Jesus turned to the man and said, "Don't be afraid; just believe."

When they reached the man's house, Jesus saw people sad and crying because the little girl had died. But Jesus told them that the girl was not dead, she was just sleeping.

He went into her room, took her hand, and said in the language Jesus spoke, which was Aramaic, "Talitha koum!" which means, "Little girl, I say to you, get up!"

And guess what? The little girl opened her eyes and stood up! Everyone was amazed and overjoyed. They could not believe their eyes. Jesus had brought her back to life!

News of this incredible **miracle** spread throughout the land, and people were even more amazed by Jesus and what he could do.

So, in this story Jesus showed his great love and power by healing a sick woman and raising a little girl from the dead. He taught us that if we have faith and believe in him, amazing things can happen.

It is a beautiful reminder that Jesus cares for us and is always ready to help us, no matter what we are going through.

Who Do You Say that I Am?
(Mark 8:27-33)

One day, Jesus and his friends were walking along, and Jesus asked them a question. He said, "Who do people say I am?" His friends replied, "Some say you are John the Baptist, and others say Elijah or one of the **prophets**."

Then Jesus asked them, "But who do you say I am?" Peter, one of Jesus' closest friends answered, "You are the Christ, the Son of the living God!"

Jesus was happy with Peter's answer and said, "Peter, you are right! God has revealed this truth to you."

After that, Jesus told his friends not to tell anyone else about him. He explained that he would have to suffer many things, be rejected by important people, and even be killed. But he also said that after three days, he would rise again.

However, Peter did not understand why Jesus would have to go through all those difficult things. So, he took Jesus aside and started to tell him that it would not happen to him. Peter loved Jesus and did not want Jesus to suffer or die.

But Jesus knew that it was part of God's plan for him to save people from their **sins**. So, he turned to Peter and said, "You do not understand God's ways. You are thinking about things from a human point of view, not from God's perspective."

Jesus wanted his friends to understand that following him might not always be easy. He told them that if they wanted to be his **disciples**, they had to be willing to give up their own desires and take up their cross (which means facing hard times or hard things) and follow him.

So, in this story, Jesus asked his friends who they thought he was, and Peter recognized him as the Son of God. But when Jesus explained that he had to suffer and die, Peter did not understand. Jesus taught them that following him means being willing to face challenges and do what God wants, even if it is hard.

The Man Who Could Not Walk (John 5:1-16)

There was a man who was very sick. He had been sick for 38 years and could not walk properly. One day Jesus, who was a very kind and loving person, saw the man lying by a pool called Bethesda.

Jesus went up to the man and asked him, "Do you want to get well?" The man told Jesus that he could not get into the pool because whenever he tried, someone else would get in before him.

Jesus felt sorry for the man and said to him, "Get up, pick up your mat, and walk." Suddenly, a **miracle** happened! The man's legs became strong, and he was able to stand up and walk!

The man was so happy and excited! He picked up his mat and started walking around, telling everyone about the amazing thing Jesus had done for him. But it was the Sabbath day, a special day for rest and worship, and some religious leaders saw the man carrying his mat. They told him it was against the rules to do any work on the Sabbath.

The man did not know who had healed him, so he told the religious leaders that the person who made him well told him to pick up his mat and walk. The leaders were upset because Jesus had healed the man on the Sabbath, which they thought was breaking the rules.

Later, Jesus found the man again and told him, "See, you are well again. Stop **sinning**, or something worse may happen to you." Jesus wanted the man to understand that he should live a good and **righteous** life.

The man was grateful for his healing and went to tell the religious leaders that it was Jesus who had healed him. The leaders were angry and started to plan ways to hurt Jesus because they did not believe in Him.

So, the story teaches us that Jesus has the power to heal people and make them well. He cares about us and wants us to be happy and healthy. It also shows us that sometimes people might not understand or believe in Jesus, but we should always be grateful for the good things he does for us.

Jesus Praises John the Baptist (Matthew 11:2-11)

Jesus' friend, John the Baptist was in prison. John sent his friends to ask Jesus a question. John was a special person who told people about Jesus and helped prepare the way for him. But at this time, John was feeling a little unsure and had some questions for Jesus.

So, John's friends went to Jesus and asked, "Are you the one we have been waiting for? Should we expect someone else?" John wanted to make sure that Jesus was the special person sent by God.

Jesus knew that John was feeling a bit uncertain, so he told John's friends to go back and tell him about all the amazing things they saw Jesus doing. Jesus healed sick people, made blind people see, and even made people who could not walk, run and jump! He told them to remind John about all these wonderful things.

Then Jesus said something special about John. He said, "Among all the people who have ever lived, there has never been anyone greater than John the Baptist." Jesus admired

John because he was a brave and strong person who spoke the truth and helped others believe in God.

    We should thank God for John the Baptist, who helped prepare the way for Jesus. John had some questions, and Jesus reassured him by reminding him of all the amazing things he was doing. Jesus also praised John and said he was a special person.

    Jesus cares about our doubts and wants us to ask questions. He encourages us when we are feeling unsure.

Jesus Calms the Storm
(Luke 8:22-25)

One day, Jesus and his **disciples** got into a boat to go across a large lake called the Sea of Galilee. Jesus was very tired, so he decided to take a nap in the back of the boat. While he was sleeping, a big storm came up. The wind blew hard, and the waves were crashing against the boat. It was a scary situation!

The **disciples** were afraid that the boat would sink, so they woke up Jesus and said, "Master, Master, we are going to drown!" Jesus got up and looked at the stormy sea. He then spoke to the wind and the waves, telling them to calm down. And you know what happened? The wind stopped blowing, and the sea became completely calm. It was amazing!

Jesus turned to his **disciples** and asked them, "Where is your faith?" He wanted them to trust in him and know that he had the power to take care of them even in the scariest situations. The **disciples** were amazed and said to each other, "Who is this man? He commands the wind and the waves, and they obey him!"

This story teaches us that Jesus has power over nature. He can calm storms and make everything peaceful. It also reminds us to have faith in Jesus, to trust in him even when things seem scary. Just like Jesus took care of his **disciples** in the storm, he takes care of us too.

The Transfiguration of Jesus (Luke 9:28-36)

One day, Jesus took three of his closest friends, Peter, James, and John up to a mountain. As they climbed, they were feeling tired and maybe a little sleepy.

When they reached the top, Jesus began to change. His face started to shine bright, and his clothes became dazzling white, even whiter than any washing machine could make them. It was like he was glowing!

Suddenly, two special people appeared beside Jesus. They were Moses, who was an important leader from long ago, and Elijah, a famous **prophet**. Peter, James, and John were amazed and excited to see them.

The three friends could not believe their eyes! Peter, who always had something to say, suggested building three little tents for Jesus, Moses, and Elijah so they could stay on the mountain forever. But as he was speaking, a bright cloud came over them, and a voice from the cloud said, "This is my Son, whom I love. Listen to him!"

The friends were terrified and fell to the ground. But Jesus came and touched them, saying, "Get up! Do not be afraid." When they looked up, Moses and Elijah were gone, and they saw only Jesus.

As they went back down the mountain, Jesus told them not to tell anyone what they had seen until he had been raised from the dead. The friends did not really understand what Jesus meant, but they knew it was something very important.

So, this story tells us that Jesus is very special. God wanted to show Peter, James, and John just how amazing Jesus was so he let them see his **glory**. It is a reminder for us to listen to Jesus and remember that he is God's Son, and he has a plan for us.

Jesus Teaches His Friends How to Pray (Luke 11:1-13)

Jesus was talking to his friends, and they asked him to teach them how to pray. So, Jesus taught them a special prayer we call the Lord's Prayer. It goes like this:

"Father, may Your name be kept holy.

May Your kingdom come.

Give us each day the food we need.

Forgive us our **sins**,

as we forgive those who **sin** against us.

And do not let us give in to temptation."

Jesus wanted them to know that they could talk to God, who is like their loving Father. He encouraged them to show respect and honor to God's name. He also reminded them to pray for God's kingdom to come and for God's will to be done on earth, just like it is done in heaven.

Jesus understood that we need food to live, so he told his friends to ask God for their daily bread, which means asking for the things they need to eat every day.

Then, Jesus talked about forgiveness. He said that if we do something wrong or hurt someone, we should ask God for forgiveness. But Jesus also said that we should forgive others who hurt us, just like God forgives us when we make mistakes.

Lastly, Jesus talked about resisting temptation. He told his friends to ask God for strength to stay away from things that are not good for them and to make wise choices.

Jesus then explained that God is like a loving parent who wants to give good things to his children. He compared it to a child asking their father for bread. A loving father would never give their child a stone instead of bread or a snake instead of a fish. In the same way, God wants to give us good things when we ask him.

So, Jesus was teaching his friends that prayer is a way to talk to God, to ask for what we need, to seek forgiveness, to forgive others, and to ask for help in making good choices. He wanted them to know that God loves them and wants to help them in every part of their lives.

Remember, even as a child, you can talk to God and ask him for anything. He is always there to listen and help.

Jesus Blesses the Children (Mark 10:13-16)

One time some parents brought their children to see Jesus. The parents wanted Jesus to **bless** their children and spend time with them. But the **disciples**, who were Jesus' helpers, tried to stop the children from coming near Jesus because they thought he was too busy for children.

When Jesus saw what was happening, he became upset with the **disciples**. He said to them, "Let the children come to me, and do not stop them, because children are important in the world where God is King." Jesus wanted the children to be close to him and experience his love.

Then, Jesus took the children in his arms, and he **blessed** them. He wanted them to know that they were important to him and to God. He said that everyone should be like children in order to live in the world where God is King. Jesus loved the children because they were innocent, trusting, and full of wonder.

Jesus cares about children and wants them to be close to him. It also reminds us that we should approach God with childlike faith and trust. Just like the children in the story, we can come to Jesus, ask for his **blessings** and know that he loves us very much.

A Question of Greatness (Mark 35-45)

There were two brothers named James and John who followed Jesus. They loved Jesus very much and believed that he was very important.

One day, James and John had a special request for Jesus. They went up to him and said, "Teacher, we want to ask you something. Can we sit beside you in your special place when you become king?"

Jesus looked at them kindly and said, "You do not really understand what you are asking. Sitting next to me in my kingdom is not for me to decide. It is for God to decide."

Jesus then explained to them that being close to him and being important in his kingdom was not about sitting in fancy chairs or being better than others. He told them, "If you want to be great and important in my kingdom, you must be willing to serve others and help them."

He went on to say, "I came not to be served, but to serve others and give my life to save many people. If you want to be truly great, you must be willing to serve and help others too."

Jesus wanted James and John, as well as all his other followers to understand that true greatness comes from showing kindness, love, and care to others. It is not about being bossy or wanting all the attention for yourself.

When the other **disciples** heard about James and John's request, they became a little upset. They thought James and John were trying to be more important than everyone else. But Jesus gathered all of them together and explained again that in his kingdom, the greatest people are the ones who are humble and willing to serve.

He told them, "Whoever wants to be the greatest among you must become like a servant, and whoever wants to be first must be the servant of all. Even I did not come to be served, but to serve others and give my life for them."

The **disciples** started to understand that Jesus was teaching them a valuable lesson about putting others first and being kind to everyone. James and John were learning that being great does not mean being better than others, but it means being helpful, caring, and serving others with a kind heart, just like Jesus did.

Jesus Feeds 5000 People
(John 6:1-14)

One day, Jesus and his friends were walking by a big lake. A lot of people started following Jesus because they had heard amazing things about him and wanted to see the wonderful things he did.

When Jesus saw all the people, he felt love and compassion for them. He knew they were hungry, so he turned to his friend Philip and asked, "Where can we buy enough food for all these people to eat?"

Philip was a little worried because they did not have a lot of money to buy food for so many people. But then another friend, Andrew, spoke up. He said, "There is a little boy here who has five small loaves of bread and two fish. But that will not be enough for everyone."

Jesus told everyone to sit down on the grass. He took the loaves of bread and fish from the little boy and looked up to heaven. He thanked God for the food and started to break it into pieces.

Then, something amazing happened! The small amount of food suddenly became enough! There was enough for everyone to eat. Jesus' friends started passing out the food to the people, and they all ate until their stomachs were full.

After everyone had eaten, Jesus asked his friends to gather up the leftovers. They collected twelve baskets full of bread and fish. From two fish and two small loaves of bread to twelve baskets of leftovers!

The people who saw this **miracle** were amazed. They realized that Jesus was not just an ordinary person but someone very special. They knew that God had done something incredible through him.

This story teaches us that when we give what we have, even if it seems small, and trust in God, he can do amazing things. Jesus showed us that we should care for others and share what we have with them. Just like the little boy who gave his bread and fish, we can help others and trust that God will take care of us too.

So, remember no matter how small you think your kindness or generosity is, it can make a big difference in someone's life, just like the little boy's lunch did for all those people that day.

Jesus Heals a Man Born Blind (John 9:1-38)

There was a man who was born blind, which means he could not see anything his whole life. He never saw the bright colors of flowers or the smiles on people's faces.

One day, Jesus came to the man's town. People told Jesus about the man and his blindness. Jesus felt a lot of love and compassion for him, so he wanted to help him.

Jesus did something very unusual. He spit on the ground and made mud with his saliva. Then he spread the mud on the man's eyes. Jesus told him to go and wash the mud off in a pool of water called Siloam.

The man listened to Jesus and went to the pool. He dipped his hands into the water and washed his eyes clean. Suddenly, something incredible happened! He could see! He blinked his eyes, and the world around him became bright and beautiful. He saw the trees, the sky, and the people. The man born blind was no longer blind. He was so happy!

News about the **miracle** spread quickly, and everyone in the town was amazed. People could not believe that the man who was once blind, could now see. They wanted to know how this wonderful thing happened to him.

Some people did not believe it was really him. They thought he must be someone else who just looked like him. So, they asked the man, "Is it really you? How did this happen?"

The man happily replied, "Yes, it is me! Jesus healed me. He made mud and put it on my eyes, and then I washed it off in the pool of water. Now I can see!"

The people could not believe their ears. They wanted to know more, so they brought the man to the religious leaders of the town. They asked him the same questions, and he told them the same story about Jesus healing him.

But the religious leaders were not happy. They were jealous of Jesus and did not want him to become more popular. They did not believe that Jesus had the power to heal people. They even called Jesus a **sinner**.

The leaders called the man's parents and asked them, "Is this your son? Was he really born blind?"

The man's parents confirmed that he was indeed their son and that he was born blind. But they were afraid of the leaders, so they did not want to say much more.

Again, they asked him, "How did this happen? What did Jesus do to you?"

The man patiently explained, "I already told you. Jesus put mud on my eyes, and when I washed it off, I could see!"

The religious leaders did not want to accept that something amazing had happened. They did not want to believe in Jesus. They got angry with the man and said, "You're one of Jesus' followers now! We do not want anything to do with you!"

Jesus heard about what happened and found the man. He asked him, "Do you believe in the **Son of Man**?"

The man happily replied, "Who is he, sir? I want to believe in him."

Jesus smiled and said, "You have seen him. It is me—Jesus, the one who healed you."

The man fell down before Jesus and said, "Lord, I believe!" He was filled with joy because he now believed in Jesus, the one who had given him sight.

Jesus Raises His Friend Lazarus (John 11:1-44)

Jesus had many friends. He had three special friends: Mary, Martha, and Lazarus. They were sisters and brother. One day, Jesus received some sad news about Lazarus. He was very sick, and his sisters were worried about him.

Jesus loved Lazarus and his sisters very much, so he decided to go and visit them. But there was a problem. Jesus did not leave right away to go see his friend. When Jesus and his **disciples** arrived in the town where Lazarus lived, Lazarus had died and was buried in a cave called a tomb. Lazarus had been in the tomb for four days. Martha and Mary were filled with sadness and many people from the town came to comfort them.

When Martha heard that Jesus had come, she went out to meet him. She told Jesus that if he had been there earlier, he could have healed him and Lazarus would not have died. But Jesus told her something amazing. He said, "I am the **resurrection** and the life. Those who believes in me will live, even though they die."

Mary also came to see Jesus, and she was crying along with the people who came to support them. Jesus saw their sadness, and it made him very sad too. He asked them to take him to the tomb where Lazarus was buried.

When they reached the tomb, Jesus asked people to remove the stone that covered the entrance. Then, Jesus prayed to God and called out with a loud voice, "Lazarus, come out!" And guess what happened next? Lazarus, who was once dead came out of the tomb! He was alive again!

Everyone was filled with amazement and joy. Jesus had performed a **miracle**! He brought Lazarus back to life! It was a wonderful moment for Lazarus, Mary, Martha, and all the people who witnessed this **miracle**.

Jesus has the power to bring life even to those who have died. It teaches us that we can trust in Jesus and believe in him because he is the source of life and hope. Just like Jesus brought Lazarus back to life, he can bring us hope, comfort, and eternal life too.

Ten Bridesmaids and Their Lamps (Matthew 25:1-13).

There were ten friends who loved to celebrate special occasions together. They were excitedly waiting for a grand wedding to happen, and they all wanted to join in the festivities. These friends had a special task: they were bridesmaids and each of them was given a lamp to carry. The lamp was like a candle that used oil instead of electricity. Carrying the lamp would light up their way and welcome the bridegroom when he arrived.

Five of the friends were very wise. They made sure to bring extra oil for their lamps, just in case they burned out. They were prepared and ready to light up the night.

The other five friends, though they were excited too, did not bring any extra oil with them. They thought the oil they had in their lamps would be enough for the whole celebration. But they did not know how long they would have to wait for the bridegroom to arrive.

As the sun began to set, the friends grew tired and decided to rest for a while. Eventually, they all fell asleep. Suddenly, in the middle of the night someone shouted,

"Look, the bridegroom is coming! Let us light up our lamps and welcome him!"

The five wise friends quickly grabbed their lamps, and they had plenty of oil to light them up. Their lamps shone brightly and illuminated the way. They were ready to join the joyful procession and greet the bridegroom.

However, the five friends who did not bring extra oil realized that their lamps were running out of light. They panicked and asked the others for some oil, saying, "Please give us some of your oil. Our lamps are going out!"

The wise friends, wanting to help, replied, "We would love to share with you, but we might not have enough for all of us. It is better if you go and buy some oil for yourselves."

So, the five friends who had not prepared went off to buy more oil, hoping they could make it back in time. But while they were away, the bridegroom arrived, and those who were ready went inside with him to enjoy the celebration. The door was closed, and the other five friends who were late missed out on the joyous occasion.

When they returned with their newly purchased oil, they found themselves locked out. They knocked on the door and cried out,

"Please, let us in!" But it was too late. The bridegroom replied, "Truly I tell you, I do not know you."

The five friends who were not prepared were very sad and disappointed. They had not realized the importance of being ready and the need to bring extra oil for their lamps. They missed out on the wedding feast and the happiness that came with it.

We need to be prepared and ready for important things in life and to be ready for Jesus when he returns to earth a second time to take away everyone's pain and sadness. We do that by living our lives in obedience to him. Just like the wise friends who brought extra oil, we should be responsible and plan ahead. Whether it is studying for a test, finishing our homework, cleaning our room or being ready for a special occasion, being prepared helps us make the most of opportunities that come our way. Being ready for the daily things in life remind us to live as Jesus did, so we can be ready when he comes again.

The Sheep and the Goats (Matthew 25:31-46)

Jesus said that one day he will come back to Earth and sit on a big, beautiful throne. And when he does, all the people from everywhere will gather in front of him. He will separate them into two groups, just like a shepherd separates the sheep from the goats.

To the group on his right, Jesus will say, "You are like my sheep. You have been kind and helpful to others, just like how you would take care of me." He will tell them that when they saw someone who was hungry, they gave them food to eat. When someone was thirsty, they gave them something to drink. When someone did not have any clothes, they gave them clothes to wear. They even visited people who were sick and in prison. Jesus will be so happy with them and say that they are like family to him.

But to the group on his left, Jesus will say, "You are like the goats. You did not help others when they needed it, just like you did not help me." He will tell them that when someone was hungry, they did not give them any food. When someone was thirsty, they did not give them a drink. When someone needed clothes, they did not give them any. And they did not visit people who were sick or in prison. Jesus will be sad because they did not show love and kindness to others.

Then, Jesus will say to the sheep, "You will have a wonderful place with me in heaven, where there is joy and love forever." But to the goats, He will say, "You will not come to heaven with me because you did not help others." Heaven is a place where people help and love people.

So, the lesson from this story is that Jesus wants us to be kind and help people when they need it. When we show love to others, it is like we are showing love to Jesus himself. When we care for others and do good things for them, we are really doing it for Jesus. And when we do these things, we will have a special place in heaven with Jesus, where we will be happy forever.

Remember, being kind to others is one of the most important things we can do, just like Jesus taught us.

Mary Anoints Jesus' Feet
(John 12:1-8)

One day, Jesus went to visit his friends, Mary, Martha & Lazarus, in a little town called Bethany. Lazarus was the friend who died and Jesus raised from the dead.

When Jesus arrived at their house, they were all very happy to see him. They prepared a special dinner for Jesus to show their love and respect. Martha, the sister who loved taking care of things, worked hard to make sure everything was perfect. She cooked delicious food and made sure the house was clean and tidy.

While Martha was busy, her sister Mary had a different idea. She had brought something very precious to her. Mary took out a bottle of expensive perfume. It smelled so good! She poured the perfume on Jesus' feet and started wiping them with her hair. The whole room filled with the wonderful fragrance of the perfume.

Some of the other people in the room saw what Mary was doing and became upset. They thought Mary was wasting the expensive perfume. They said, "You should have sold the perfume and given the money to the poor! It could have helped so many people!'

But Jesus understood Mary's heart. He knew that she loved him and wanted to show her gratitude. Jesus said to the people, "Leave her alone. She has done a beautiful thing for me. You will always have the poor among you, but you will not always have me."

Jesus explained that Mary's act of love was more important than the money they could have received for the perfume. He knew that the perfume was special to her, and she gave it to him willingly because she loved him so much.

Jesus wanted everyone to understand that acts of love and kindness are precious, just like the perfume. Sometimes we might have something special, and we feel like sharing it with someone we love. It is not about the money or things we have, but about showing our love and appreciation for one another.

This story teaches us that it is important to show love and gratitude to those we care about, even if it means giving something precious. Jesus valued Mary's act of love and reminds us to cherish acts of kindness and love in our own lives.

A Big Parade! (John 12:12-19)

One day, Jesus decided to go on a journey to a city called Jerusalem. When the people heard that Jesus was coming, they became very excited. They ran to find palm branches and waved them in the air. They also spread their coats on the ground to make a special path for Jesus. They shouted, "Hooray! Jesus is coming!"

Jesus rode into the city on a donkey, which was a humble and gentle animal. The people were so happy to see Jesus that they thought he was going to be their king! They believed he would be the one to save them and make everything better.

The crowd followed Jesus and cheered for him as he went through the city. They sang songs and praised him. The excitement was everywhere!

Some of the religious leaders, called the Pharisees, saw all of this and became worried. They did not like that the people were following Jesus and thought he might become too powerful. They did not understand that Jesus came to bring love and forgiveness to everyone.

But Jesus did not let the Pharisees' worries bother him. He continued on his way, spreading his message of love and hope.

The people who believed in him were so happy to be with him and learn from him.

So, that is the story of Jesus entering Jerusalem. It is a story of joy and excitement, where people welcomed Jesus with open hearts. It reminds us that we can also welcome Jesus into our lives and follow his teachings of love, kindness, and forgiveness.

Jesus Washes his Disciples' Feet (John 13:1-20)

One day, Jesus and his friends gathered together for a special meal called the Passover.

Jesus knew that something important was going to happen, so he decided to show his friends how much he loved them. He took off his outer clothes and wrapped a towel around his waist, just like a servant. Then he poured some water into a bowl.

Jesus went to his friends one by one and started washing their feet with the water. In those days, people used to walk on dusty roads and their feet would get very dirty. Washing feet was a job for servants, but Jesus wanted to show his friends that he was willing to do even the lowliest tasks to show his love for them.

When Jesus came to his friend Peter, Peter did not understand why Jesus wanted to wash his feet. He thought it should be the other way around. But Jesus told Peter that if he did not let Jesus wash his feet, then Peter would not be a part of what Jesus was doing.

Peter quickly realized that Jesus was not just washing their feet to make them clean. He was teaching them an important lesson about **humility** and serving others. Jesus wanted them to love and serve one another, just as he had loved and served them.

After Jesus finished washing their feet, he put his clothes back on and sat down with his friends again. He explained to them that he had set an example for them to follow. He said, "I have given you an example, that you should do as I have done to you."

Jesus wanted his friends to understand that being great did not mean being the most important or powerful. It meant being willing to serve others and show them love and kindness.

Jesus knew that one of his friends, Judas, was going to betray him and hand him over to his enemies. But even so, Jesus still loved Judas and washed his feet too. Jesus wanted to show Judas that he was loved, even though he was going to do something wrong.

Jesus finished talking to his friends and said, "I tell you the truth, no servant is greater than his master, nor is a messenger greater than the one who sent him." He wanted them to remember that they should follow his example and love and serve one another, just as he had loved and served them.

The Last Supper (Mark 14:12-32)

Jesus and his **disciples** were getting ready to celebrate a special meal called the Passover. Jesus knew his death was coming, so it would be the last supper he would eat with them. They needed to find a place to have the meal together, so Jesus told two of his **disciples** to go into the city. He told them they would see a man carrying a jar of water, and they should follow him. When they found the man, they were to go to the house he entered and ask the owner if they could use a room for the meal.

So, the two **disciples** did exactly as Jesus had said, and they found the man and the house just as Jesus had described. They prepared everything for the Passover meal, and when evening came, Jesus and the other **disciples** arrived.

During the meal, Jesus did something very special. He took a piece of bread, gave thanks to God, and broke it into pieces. He then gave a piece to each of his **disciples** and said, "Take this bread, it represents my body."

Afterward, Jesus took a cup of wine and gave thanks to God. He passed the cup to his **disciples** and said, "Drink from it, all of you. This cup represents my blood, which will be poured out to forgive people's **sins**."

Jesus explained to his **disciples** that the bread and the cup were symbols of a new covenant or agreement between God and people. He told them that whenever they ate the bread and drank from the cup, they should remember him and his death on the cross for their **sins**.

The important thing to remember is that Jesus shared a special meal with his **disciples**, where he showed them the bread and the cup as symbols of his body and blood. He asked them to remember him whenever they eat and drink these things. It reminds us of Jesus' love for us.

That is why the followers of Jesus celebrate Holy Communion to this day.

Jesus Is Betrayed, Arrested, Denied, and Put on Trial (Luke 22:39-23:25)

After the Last Supper, Jesus went to a place called the Mount of Olives to pray. He knew something difficult was going to happen soon.

While Jesus was praying, his **disciples** fell asleep. When Jesus woke them up, he saw that soldiers were coming to take him away. These soldiers were working for the leaders who did not like Jesus.

One of Jesus' **disciples**, named Judas had agreed to help the leaders capture Jesus. He kissed Jesus to show the soldiers who they should arrest.

The soldiers took Jesus to the leaders, and they asked him questions. But Jesus did not say anything to defend himself. The leaders accused him of saying things against their rules and claimed that he was a king. They wanted to punish him.

While Jesus was under arrest, Jesus' friend Peter followed from a distance. People started recognizing Peter and saying, "Hey, you are one of Jesus' **disciples**, right?" They were trying to see if Peter would admit that he knew Jesus.

The first time someone asked Peter, he got scared and said, "No, I do not know Him. You are mistaken." Then, a little while later another person said, "I am sure I have seen you with Jesus before!' Again, Peter denied knowing Jesus, feeling even more afraid.

Finally, a third person said, "I am positive you are one of his followers. Your accent (that's the way someone talks) gives you away!" This time, Peter became very scared and upset. He did not want to get into trouble, so he denied knowing Jesus once more. Just as Jesus had said would happen at his last supper, Peter denied him three times.

After the third denial, something remarkable happened.

Peter heard a rooster crowing, and it reminded him of what Jesus had told him earlier. Peter felt terrible and realized he had let his friend down. He started crying because he knew he had made a big mistake.

Then, the leaders took Jesus to the governor whose name was Pilate. Pilate asked Jesus if he was a king, but Jesus said that his kingdom was not like the kingdoms on Earth. Pilate did not know what to think of Jesus, but he was afraid of what the leaders might do.

Pilate discovered that Jesus was from a place called Galilee, so he sent him to King Herod, who was the ruler of that region. Herod asked Jesus many questions, but Jesus did not answer him. Herod's soldiers made fun of Jesus and treated him badly.

After a while, Herod sent Jesus back to Pilate. Pilate was not sure Jesus had done anything wrong, but he did not really care about Jesus. He did not like the religious leaders who wanted Jesus dead, so he did not want to give them what they wanted. But the leaders and the people started shouting for Jesus to be **crucified**. Pilate was afraid of the people's anger, so he gave in and allowed Jesus to be **crucified**.

Jesus Is Crucified on a Cross (Matthew 27:27-61)

After Jesus' trial, a group of soldiers took Jesus away to a place called the Governor's Palace. There, they gathered all the soldiers together and they made fun of Jesus. They put a special robe on him and made a crown out of thorns. They pretended he was a king and started teasing him. They even spit on him and hit him.

After they were done making fun of Jesus, the soldiers took him to a place called Golgotha, which means "the place of the skull." They put three crosses on top of the hill. Two criminals were being punished on the crosses next to Jesus.

While Jesus was hanging on the cross, some people who did not like him passed by and made fun of him. They said mean things and even challenged him, saying, "If you're really the Son of God, save yourself!"

But Jesus knew his purpose. He stayed on the cross and forgave those who were hurting him. He loved them even though they were being mean to him. He looked down and saw his mother and his close friend standing nearby. He wanted to make sure they would be taken care of, so he asked his friend to look after his mother.

As the day went on, the sky became dark, and it felt like something very important was happening. Jesus cried out in a loud voice and took his last breath. At that moment, the earth shook, and the Temple curtain (which separated God from the people) tore in two, showing that now God and the people would be together because of Jesus. They would never be separated again.

There was a kind man named Joseph of Arimathea who loved Jesus. He went to the governor and asked for Jesus' body. Joseph, along with some others took Jesus down from the cross and wrapped his body in a clean cloth. They placed him in a tomb, which was like a big cave, and rolled a big stone in front of the entrance.

Jesus' friends were sad and confused. They did not understand why Jesus had to die. But little did they know that something unexpected was about to happen.

So, even though this part of the story is sad, it is important to remember that Jesus gave his life because he loves us so much. And his love is something we can always hold on to no matter what happens.

Jesus is Alive Again! (Mark 16:1-8)

After Jesus was arrested and **crucified** on a cross, his friends and followers were heartbroken. They thought all hope was lost. But something amazing was about to happen.

After Jesus was buried in a tomb, three women named Mary Magdalene, Mary the mother of James, and Salome, wanted to visit the tomb early in the morning on the third day. They brought spices to honor Jesus and were worried about how they would move the big stone covering the tomb's entrance.

As they walked to the tomb, the women wondered who would help them. But when they arrived, they saw something incredible! The huge stone had been rolled away, and the tomb was empty. Jesus was not there!

Suddenly, they saw a young man dressed in white clothes inside the tomb. He said to them, "Do not be afraid! I know you are looking for Jesus who was **crucified**. He is not here. He has risen from the dead! Go and tell his **disciples**, including Peter, that Jesus is going ahead of you to Galilee. You will see him there, just as he told you."

The Risen Jesus Appears to Two Disciples (Luke 24:13-35)

After Jesus had been raised from the dead, two of his followers were walking on a road to a village called Emmaus. These two friends did not know yet that Jesus was alive, though they heard some rumors about it. They were feeling very sad and confused because they thought Jesus was the promised **Savior**, but now he was gone. As they walked, they talked about all the things that had happened.

Suddenly, a stranger came up and started walking with them. They did not recognize him because their eyes were kept from seeing who he really was. The stranger asked them, "What are you talking about?" The two followers stopped walking and looked sad. One of them named Cleopas replied, "Are you the only person in Jerusalem who does not know what just happened? Our friend Jesus, who we thought was the **Savior** was **crucified**, and now his tomb is empty. Some of our women friends say that he is alive again, but that seems too good to be true."

The stranger looked at them kindly and said, "Oh, foolish ones! Don't you understand? Everything that was written about the

Savior had to come true. Let me explain." And starting with the beginning of the **Old Testament** book of Genesis and continuing to the last book of Malachi, the stranger began to teach them from the Bible, telling them about God's plan and how those prophecies came true in Jesus.

As they listened to the stranger's words, their hearts began to feel warm and hopeful. They were amazed by his knowledge and **wisdom**. The stranger's words gave them comfort and everything started to make sense.

When they reached the village, the two followers asked the stranger to stay with them because it was getting late. They sat down to eat, and the stranger took bread, gave thanks, broke it, and started giving it to them. Suddenly, their eyes were opened, and they recognized him. It was Jesus! But before they could say anything, He disappeared from their sight.

Filled with excitement and joy, the two followers said to each other, "Did not our hearts burn within us as he talked with us on the road and explained the Scriptures?" They could not contain their happiness, so they got up immediately and rushed back to Jerusalem, where the other **disciples** were gathered.

When they arrived, they found the **disciples** and others saying, "The Lord has risen indeed! He has appeared to the **disciple** Peter!" The two followers then shared their own incredible experience of meeting Jesus on the road to Emmaus and how he revealed himself to them as they broke bread together.

When we feel sad or confused, Jesus is always with us ready to help us understand and find hope. He is the **Savior** who fulfills God's plan and brings us joy. Just like the two followers, we can have our hearts filled with warmth and happiness when we spend time with Jesus and listen to His words.

Jesus Ascends to Heaven (Acts 1:6-11)

After Jesus rose from the dead, He spent some time with his **disciples**, teaching them and showing them that he was alive. They were filled with joy and hope because they knew that Jesus was the **Savior** sent by God.

One day, Jesus gathered his **disciples** together on a hillside and they asked him an important question. They said, "Lord, is it now the time when you will restore the place where God is King?"

But Jesus had a special plan in mind. He told them, "It is not for you to know the times or dates set by the Heavenly Father. But you will receive power when the Holy Spirit comes on you, and you will be my witnesses in Jerusalem, and in all Judea, and Samaria, and to the ends of the earth."

Jesus wanted his **disciples** to understand that they had a big job to do. He wanted them to spread the good news about him to people everywhere, starting in Jerusalem and reaching the farthest corners of the earth. Jesus promised them that the Holy Spirit would come and give them the power they needed to fulfill this important task.

After saying these things, something incredible happened. While the **disciples** were still looking up at Jesus, he began to rise into the sky! They watched in awe as Jesus went higher and higher until a cloud hid him from their sight.

As the **disciples** were standing there trying to understand what had just happened, two **angels** appeared beside them. The **angels** said, "Men of Galilee (that is where the **disciples** were from), why do you stand looking into heaven? This Jesus, who was taken up from you into heaven, will come in the same way as you saw him go into heaven."

The **disciples** were amazed and filled with joy. They knew that Jesus was going to come back again someday, just as he had promised. They realized that their mission was to share the good news of Jesus with others until that day came.

So, the disciples went back to Jerusalem, filled with hope and excitement. They gathered together and prayed, waiting for the Holy Spirit to come and give them the power to be witnesses for Jesus. The Holy Spirit is God's special person, giving his special presence to them. And when the Holy Spirit came, they were filled with boldness and began to tell everyone about Jesus, starting in Jerusalem and spreading out to the ends of the earth, just as Jesus had commanded them.

Jesus has given us the Holy Spirit. He has given us an important mission too—to share his love and good news with others, and to eagerly wait for his return.

Glossary

Angels: Angels are beings that live in heaven with God. The word "angel" means messenger. They take messages from God to people on earth like the angel Gabriel took the message to Mary that she was going to give birth to Jesus.

Anoint, Anointing: When someone is anointed that means they have something special to do for God. Jesus was God's Anointed because his special task was to offer salvation to the world.

Apostle: The word "apostle" means one who is sent. Jesus' first twelve followers are called apostles because Jesus sent them into the world to tell the Good News of God's love in Jesus.

Baptism, Baptized: When people are baptized, they are put under the water or water is put on their heads. The water symbolizes that they are now part of God's family and that God forgives their sins.

Bless, Blessing: To be blessed is to be given something special. It's like a gift. God gives us many blessings like people who love us and food to eat.

Crucifixion, Crucify: In Jesus' world crucifixion was a way of killing people. It was a terrible way to die. The people in power would put two pieces of wood shaped like a **T** in the ground and they would hang the person on it. Jesus died on the cross for our sins. I know how terrible that sounds, but Jesus died for us so that no one else would ever have to die like that again.

Disciple: A disciple is a follower of someone. To be a disciple of Jesus is to follow him by loving God and people, and by listening to his teaching.

Glory: The word glory is way of referring to God as special and like no one else.

Humility: To be humble is to know that while you are special, you are not more special than anyone else. God loves everyone as much as God loves you. People who are not humble think they are better than others.

Inherit: An inheritance is when someone leaves their money and what they own to loved ones. Children inherit their parents' possessions after they die. To say that God gives us an inheritance is to know that God loves us so much he has given us everything in this world to enjoy and most of all he has given us the inheritance of going to heaven because of Jesus.

Mercy: To show mercy to someone is to be kind to them even if they haven't been kind to you.

Miracle: A miracle is something special that only God can do and we cannot understand how God did it.

Old Testament: The Old Testament is the first half (well, more than half) of the Bible. It begins with the book of Genesis and ends with the book of Malachi with lots of books in between. The New Testament comes after that. It begins with the Gospel of Matthew and ends with the book of Revelation with many books in between.

Prophet: A prophet is someone who speaks for God.

Rejoice: To rejoice is to be happy even in difficult times because you know God is with you.

Resurrection: When someone is resurrected, they come back from the dead and are alive again. Resurrection is a miracle only God can do.

Righteous: When someone is righteous, they are living a life that pleases God, obeying his Word and living like Jesus.

Savior: To save someone is to rescue them like a firefighter rescues someone from a burning building. Jesus is our Savior because he rescues us from our sin.

Sin: Sin is something we do that Jesus would not do. If Jesus wouldn't do it, neither should we.

Son of Man: Jesus is the Son of Man. It refers to the fact that Jesus is God's real presence with us.

Wisdom: Wisdom in the Bible refers to people who know the ways of God and what God expects.